Pebble™ Plus

Under the Sea

Sea Stars

by Jody Sullivan

Consulting Editor: Gail Saunders-Smith, PhD

Consultant: Debbie Nuzzolo, Education Manager
SeaWorld, San Diego, California

Capstone *press*

Mankato, Minnesota

Pebble Plus is published by Capstone Press,
151 Good Counsel Drive, P.O. Box 669, Mankato, Minnesota 56002.
www.capstonepress.com

1 2 3 4 5 6 10 09 08 07 06 05

Library of Congress Cataloging-in-Publication Data
Sullivan, Jody.
   Sea stars / by Jody Sullivan.
   p. cm.—(Pebble plus. Under the sea)
   Summary: "Simple text and photographs present sea stars, where they live, how they
look, and what they do"—Provided by publisher.
   Includes bibliographical references and index.
   ISBN 0-7368-4272-1 (hardcover)
   1. Starfishes—Juvenile literature. I. Title. II. Series: Under the sea (Mankato, Minn.)
QL384.A8S845 2006
593.9'3—dc22   2004026905

Editorial Credits
Martha E. H. Rustad and Aaron Sautter, editors; Juliette Peters, set designer; Kate Opseth, book designer;
   Kelly Garvin, photo researcher; Scott Thoms, photo editor

Photo Credits
Corbis/Stuart Westmorland, 4–5
Dwight R. Kuhn, 15
Herb Segars, 17, 18–19
Jeff Rotman, 11
Marty Snyderman, 1, 12–13
Minden Pictures/Fred Bavendam, cover
Seapics.com/Celeste Fowler, 6–7; James D. Watt, 9, 20–21

Note to Parents and Teachers

The Under the Sea set supports national science standards related to the diversity and
unity of life. This book describes and illustrates sea stars. The images support early
readers in understanding the text. The repetition of words and phrases helps early
readers learn new words. This book also introduces early readers to subject-specific
vocabulary words, which are defined in the Glossary section. Early readers may need
assistance to read some words and to use the Table of Contents, Glossary, Read More,
Internet Sites, and Index sections of the book.

Table of Contents

What Are Sea Stars?

Sea stars are sea animals.

They have rough, bumpy skin.

Large sea stars are
about the size
of a bicycle wheel.
Small sea stars are
about the size of a quarter.

Body Parts

Sea stars have five or more
arms called rays.

ray

Sea stars have tiny feet
shaped like tubes.
Many strong feet
cover the bottom
of each ray.

foot

What Sea Stars Do

Sea stars move slowly.
They grip coral reefs and
rocks with their feet.

Sea stars sometimes
lose their rays.
They grow new rays.

new ray

Sea stars eat

plants and animals.

Sea stars open clams

with their feet.

Sea stars push their stomachs
into clam shells.
Then they eat the clams.

stomach

Under the Sea

Sea stars can be
many different colors.

Sea stars live under the sea.

Glossary

clam—an animal that lives inside a shell; a sea star pushes its stomach out of its mouth and into a clam's shell to eat the clam.

coral reef—an area of coral skeletons and rocks in shallow ocean water

grip—to hold something tightly

ray—an arm of a sea star; sea stars use tiny feet on rays to move and to hold food.

stomach—a body part where food is digested

tube—a round, hollow shape that is open at both ends; a sea star's feet are shaped like tubes.

Read More

Blaxland, Beth. *Sea Stars, Sea Urchins, and Their Relatives: Echinoderms.* Invertebrates. Philadelphia: Chelsea House, 2003.

Hirschmann, Kris. *Sea Stars.* Creatures of the Sea. San Diego: KidHaven Press/Thomson Gale, 2003.

Zuchora-Walske, Christine. *Spiny Sea Stars.* Pull Ahead Books. Minneapolis: Lerner, 2001.

Internet Sites

FactHound offers a safe, fun way to find Internet sites related to this book. All of the sites on FactHound have been researched by our staff.

Here's how:

1. Visit *www.facthound.com*

2. Type in this special code **0736842721** for age-appropriate sites. Or enter a search word related to this book for a more general search.

3. Click on the **Fetch It** button.

FactHound will fetch the best sites for you!

Index

Word Count: 119
Grade: 1
Early-Intervention Level: 14